Parts

of

MAN

The Declaration
of Truth

Poems, Songs & Lyrics
by
Marwan Fateen

First Edition

5-31-14

ignigma Publishing Co.
Chicago, Illinois
blackmagazine@yahoo.com

ISBN-10: 0615787738
ISBN-13: 978-0-615-78773-2

Dedication

This book is dedicated to my neighborhood, the Roseland Communiy. My elementary school, Curtis Elementary ('88 - '96), whose teachers and faculty did the best they could with whatever resources they had, to give us a quality education. To Mrs. Ortega, Mr. Jones, my 8th grade teacher Ms. Palm (who had us recite poetry every morning and taught us etiquette and how to write as though you speak,) Mrs. Neely, Mr. Terry, Mrs. Jordan, assistant principal Mr. Hamilton and the many more who gave me hope. Those thousands of lines I had to write for punishment really helped me become proficient with the pen.

-111th st. YMCA & The Manhood Training Program ('93- '95)

-To the people I've met for the past eight years throughout Chicago, who supported my art and literature and kept me motivated and inspired to keep moving forward.

-To my friends and enemies, to 112th, 113th and 114th. The Stinson family. My family; my mother and father who stayed married and did their best to provide for twelve children without government support. My mother with her constant home school lessons. My siblings for being about educations and advancement through knowledge and excellence. My father for showing us how to be a man. To my Brother Khayree for always looking out for me.

-And to the people in the stuggle worldwide hoping for a better life and a better day, who couldn't make it this far, who fell victim to poverty, lack of education, finance, lack of jobs and opportunities, the gangs and drugs. Despite your circumstances and upbringing and enviornment, you still can achieve anything you set your mind to with determination, dedication, discipline and trust and faith in God.

This book wouldn't exist without you all.

Preface

For the last four years, I've been writing and publishing this book of poems, Parts of Man: The Declaration of Truth. It's divided into three parts: The Dark Ages, The Enlightenment, and The Renaissance. There's also a second book at the end called "The Book of Lyrics." The main idea behind Parts of Man is that man is made up of more than just flesh. You have a mind, body, soul, nationality and creed and each of those parts have endless aspects.

"the journey of the soul"

Life is the greatest inspiration for art, espcially your own personal experiences. We all may go through similar situations but we experience them our own unique way. We all have our own signature on everything we do or go through. This is what makes art so special and different. It comes from the person's individual soul, body, name, nationality, religion, and every other aspect that makes up the person. Those are the Parts of Man in which this book is based on. Each poem deals with a different situation, motivaion, intention based on my own unique experiences and thoughts. The reader must find the balance and equalibrium to connect themselves and extract the essence of this literature. Just as we go though things our own way, we also see and interpret them differently. Every reader of this book will see it based on who they are and what they've gone through. While reading this book, if you find yourself inspired to create your own lyrics, at the end there's a section called, THE FINAL Chapter, where you can write your own lyrics, poetry or literature. In essense, the last chapter of this books will be written by you, the reader. You will complete this book in your own unique way.

This book will delve into the common struggles and problems that we all face throughout life and must overcome in order to move to the next level and elevate to our divine self and realize and start living our purpose in life.

The purpose of this book is to give the reader an understanding that we humans are more than just flesh, physical animals, and that we all have a unique perpose on this planet.

It's preferred that you read this book from beginning to end but it can be read in any order or sequence. It doesn't necessary have to be read from front to back.

I want this book to be beneficial to humanity. It deals with real life situations so if you are going through a particular situation in your life, you might find a poem that speaks directly to that situation and act as a relief, a medicine, encouragement, motivaiton, or enlightenment. Look through the Contents to find what speaks to you. This book is meant to be used continously as a guide and tool throughout life to help you get through different stages and situations and to know what to do and what not to do, what works and what doesn't; such as dealing with relationships, loss, trauma, depression, joy, overcoming obstacales, perseverence, determinaitons, blessings, curses, ups, downs, love, hate, etc. With each situation, there is something to be gained before you can move on to the next stage. These. poems are some of what I've gained from those situaitons.

This book is a journey to find oneself.

Struggle is the one thing everyone has in common and our common beginning is ignorance. We struggle out of the darkness into the light. Some have it easier than others but the beauty of life is the harder you have it to get out of the darkness, the better you will become in the long run and the higher you can elevate in life. This book gives my personal struggles in artistic, poetic, lyrical form from the earlier years of my life until my current adult years. I tried to be as honest with these lyrics as possible.

-Marwan Fateen

Introduction

In the midst of all of the chaos and confusion caused by living life, man is in a constant state of change, either rising or falling, growing or decaying, happy or sad, young or old. God puts man through tests, trials and tribulations to teach him the truth about himself, reality, and life. If only we stop, analyze, examine and recognize the situaltions we're placed in and learn. This will lead to wisdom and the beginnings of wisdom, according to the Holy BIBLE, is the fear of God. Wisdom is like a tree of life. This book, Parts of Man, gives true life experience and extracts the wisdom out of each situation to elevate and enhance the readers understanding of life, themselves, and God. The more you elevate in life, the more complex the lessons and understanding. In the Holy Bible, man starts off innocent, then gets corrupted and falls, then rises from that fall, then gets refined when the earth was destroyed in the days of Noah, then man was furher refined through the develpment of high priests and prophets, then man fell again. Then man was further refined through the choosing of Abraham by God, and this is where the story really begins. His seed had to go through the greatest civilization of all time, and rose to power, got persecuted, then left. They then had to live solely off faith while resisting their temptation to go back to Egypt. After going through forty years in the wilderness, and all the members of the older generation died off, except Moses, Aaron, Joshua and Caleb, they were finally able to move to a higher level and possess the land that was promised to them. After they got this land, a period of four hundred years of rises, falls, and savoirs took place to further refine them. After the period of saviors and judges, then you had the period of Kings, starting with Saul and David to Solomon, During this period of time, God sent prophets to warn the kings of the penalty for wicked judgements and the blessings for righteousness and obedience. After this period of Kings, the Israelites were destroyed and put in captivity due to their extreme wickedness and violations against the laws of God. This period of captivity was to further refine them in order for them to appreciate what they had and to understand why they lost it. After the 70 years of captivity in Babylon, the Persians conquered Babylon and freed the Israelites and allowed them to rebuild Jerusalem. This further refined the people and preserved the seed of David in which Jesus Christ derived.

According to my beliefs, this is the process each person takes throughout their lives in order to refine who they are and figure out and accomplish their purpose on earth before leaving.

Another ancient text, the I-Ching, of ancient China, has a similar philosophy, more direct and less allegorical. The premise is humaity is a combinaiton of Heaven and Earth or Yang and Yin, or in Biblical terms, spirit and flesh, and we're in a constant state of change, from the beginning or Genesis to the end or Revelations and back to the beginning. In the I-Ching, there are 64 different states of Change that we go through. You are either coming from one and going to another. You can look through the book to figure out what state you are in to understand where you are going and see what caused it to better navigate your life. The I-Ching is a book of Divination so there's a process to figure out exactly which state of change you are in before opening the book, but the point is we all experience similar states of being or change.

In this book, Parts of Man: The Declaration of Truth, it has over 100 different poems dealing with different periods of time, with different states of mind, which can be compared to the different states of change, rising or falling, in the Bible or the I-Ching, and each state is preceded by another more different state or poem. My goal and hope is to help people who find themselves in those situations or states of change, to get out of them towards a more peaceful, positive state of existence. This will help the world as a whole become a better place to live.

In Parts of Man, there are three main orders of change, beginning, middle and ending, or knowledge, wisdom and understanding, or The Dark Ages, The Enlightenemt and The Renaissance. The Dark Ages starts the person off as dead. You're born dead due to ignorance. You start to grow once you realize you are indeed ignorant and dead and start the process of learning. In the Bible, Adam was made twice. The first time he was made on the Sixth day as flesh. Then was made the second time when he receieved the breath of life from God and became a living soul. This is the word or wisdom or the enlightenment. Once you start the process of enlightening yourself with knowledge and truth, you will be born into life, reborn or The Renaissance. After you're reborn, you start life as a child and repeat the process all over again but with a more opened mind and clearer vision. You now know right from wrong so to do wrong at this junction will insinuate an extremely wicked individual.

"What separates man from beast?"

God chose man to represent His ideals and gave him free will, the ability to think, reason, and choose. He made man in His own image and likeness. So all the aspects and parts of man are also parts of God.

The body needs food to grow, the mind needs information to grow, and the soul needs life to grow and life is wisdom and experience with a combinaiton of the mind and body in collaboration to trace the origins of thought and soul.

The renaissance means rebirth, the dark ages means death or a state of ignorance or darkness. Ignorance is the state where everyone starts. Its the common point, the equalibrium. Ignorance is truelly equality. From that we grow and learn based on our enviornment, our society and culture, our expected behaviors or expectations which our peers, our families, and society sets for us. When we start to realize the falsehoods innate in that sort of training, we then seek universal truths which transcend cultures, nations, religions, etc. That's the state of enlightenment. The search for truth; the disregard for previous notions, ideas, customs, and traditions in which no one understands but just follows based on what their forefathers practiced. We start a process of rebuilding outselves from the inside out. An interal struggle ensues between our old selves and our new and becoming self. Its hard to let go of traditions, habits, traits, and learned behaviors. Once that battle is over, if the old self still exist, you will go back to death. But, if your new self survived, you will be reborn, thus The Renaissance, the rebirth. Then you willl lead a life of enlightenment, truth, joy, happiness. You will search for pleasure in things esoteric, abstract, such as the arts, music, culture, history, science, religion, politics, etc. The mundane physical aspect of reality has lost its sway and will become secondary and a side effect of your higher pursuits at best. You will seek a soul mate to share in your journey for truth to establish justice and to shining light on the darkness, to resurrect the dead, your fellow man. This book will detail my personal and univeral struggle to that point based on differnt situations, methods, stories, life long learned lessons, struggles, heartbreak, betrayal, abandonment, near death experiences, being broke, and still holding on to something greater to keep me going further in life. Realizing that to lose is to really gain and to gain without loss is nothing. The value of wisdom, the value of knowledge, the value of doing the right thing. The reality of God and angels, demons, the esoteric unseen reality that effects us all. The different aspects of a person beyond their bodies, which makes up the majority of the individual. The millions of abstract dimensions we all inhabit at once. The virtues, the emotions, the psychology, the tastes, interests, experiences, behaviors. They are all common to every human being and are all parts of man as a whole. When things reach their extreme, their peak, according to the philosophy of the I-Ching, it will automatically produce it's opposite. So at the end of this book, you will have the opportunity to begin.

-Marwan Fateen

Contents

Part Two: The Enlightenment............................49

Part Three: The Renaissance............................87

Part One

The Dark Ages

(1) Byways & Hedges

On the byways and hedges
walking on steep ledges
hoping I don't slip and fall
and crawl
through the valley of death

gunshot are taken
dry bones and shaken
earthquakes awaken
Ain't no escaping

dark clouds are forming
ambulance & police sirens
locusts are swarming
out of the bottomless pit

what profit do I gain
to gain the world
when the world is only
a temporary manifestation
....

(2) His-Story

In the city where the gods and goddesses dwell
perpendicular to heaven, parallel to hell
ancient creeds, ancient seeds, ancient deeds
where you must have knowledge & truth to succeed
where my people, folks, & comrads call home
gangstas, scholars, revolutionaries roam

Chicago.....long way from home?
live for God or you won't last too long
that's what I told Tone
but he didn't listen
got caught up in the game
and he came up missin'
learned his lesson
no more disrespectin'
humbled his spirit
first he didn't wanna hear it
got jacked, locked up, beat then shot
now the block is too hot
can't sell his rocks
they smiled in his face
but when he turned his back
the people he associated with stole his pack
his girlfriend left him
his homeboys left him
he's all by himself
life is just messed up
NOW...he wanna change his life
lived for satan...and he paid the price
the vice, the dice, the liquor ain't cool
but at the end of the day, who's the real fool
now whats left to do
got nothin' to lose
time to choose
got somethin' to prove
what to do
walk in these shoes
leave the game....
or stay "true"
....

what would you do?

He eventually chose to change his life.. now he's back
stuck, knocked off track
with questions...
should he get a job or go back to crack?
the lesson...
not too many options with a felony conviction
took probation because it seemed like the best option
if it wasn't for drugs he'd be cool
now he gotta wait 3 years to get in school
financial aid don't honor drug charges
coulda been a pimp or robber and been better off
tried to give up the life
the drugs, the dice and vice
but its hard when you can't find a job
a decent wage of pay
they keep telling him crime don't pay
but it seems being straight don't either
prejudice, stereotype, discrimination
at least the block has equal opportunities
your hustle, skills, game and heart
was all you needed to succeed
now its your record, clothes, look and manners
that don't allow you to proceed
everywhere he goes in the city, there's enemies
they don't care if he changed
the people he robbed, beat, shot and mobbed
all remember the things he did, the gangs
he shoulda made a mends before doing the right things
because your past will catch back up with you
tried to join the consciousness movement
but when its time to move, he avoid certain hoods

they're forcin him back to a wall
his mind is changed but his heart is still there
will he fight himself or his ememies
no one will ever know
they chewed him up, spit him out
now he's on his own with nothing
you fall, get up and move on
that's the life of hustlin'
the one's he wronged are all memories to him,
but their people remember
and when they see him its on
so was the life worth it
when you can't even come home?
can't even be good, can't even live in peace
whats in it the streets, no peace for you or me
should've listened when I first tried to tell him
things probably woulda turned out better
but he learned the hard way
I hope his enemies don't get him
hope things turn out well him
because there's always a better day....
if he chooses a better way....

He got car notes, rent, child support
got fines in court
yet he don't even have a job
how is he supposed to maintain this life
without being expected to rob
you closed the doors in his face
put your hands on the mase
blocked every chance he had to do good
you wonder why people like him
are stuck in the hood?

they're no good, no misunderstood
shut out from society
you, the president, the schools, everyone all lied to me
you waited 'til his life was hell, dead or gone in jail
before you decided to show interest.
by then its too late,
now you're paid back with interest.
the people he wronged will get him
if not, God will get him, if not,
his own actions will get him
but you don't get him.
if he don't make things right today
his children won't have a bright future to stay
its better that he don't look back
and focus on all of their future
and pray

....

(3) Anger

looking for the easy way out
can't come in
because society got you brainwashed
your mind never grew
your spirit never grew
come here little brother
I'm talking to you
I'm not through
your atmosphere is too cloudy
for this light to shine through
what happened to you
when you were a little child

Frowns on your face
its hard for you to smile
it might take a while
but there is hope
all it takes is knowledge
to loosen up the rope
false ideas proclaimed about yourself
the truth will make you free
feel good about yourself
your fathers were kings
established society
without you
there is no reality
so stop looking all mad
down
its all a lie
turn that frown upside down
enjoy your life
the epitome of filth, slime
God hates the lie

they wonder why we celebrate
our Black achievements
we got held down mentally
to the pavement
erased from history
but we did our dudilligence
and discovered what was left out
it feels good
to see the good
that our people did
and withstood
everything you could

to sabotage our livelihood

(3b) Politics

On the front porch not the front line
wasting your life losing your mind
I don't have time for back in the day
what about today and tomorrow
use yesterday as a means to measure
your success or failure
Humanity
destined to struggle
walking around town
mean muggin'
got a chip on his shoulders
don't know how to use your mind
so you take
mentally crippled
society don't need you
you can't escape the burden
you don't know how to react
so you're angry
with a monkey on your back

....

(4) Demons

These demons are inside my mind
I can't escape them
they don't want me happy
they want me to suffer miserably
ruined relationships

lose my friends
I can't shake them
is being lonely my destiny
these demons come out
in my most vulnerable times
instead of showing mercy, understanding
and forgiveness
I lash out
blame and call names
without tact
I disrespect
no worries about the consequence
I can't come back
wonded souls forgive but wont forget
I'm getting old
no family or friends to spend time with
because these demons take over my soul
and I do regret
please Lord
help me get over these demons
they keep plotting and scheming
attacking while I'm dreaming

lying down at night
open my eyes
portals closing
angels exposing
I'm chosen
spirits creeping
demons seeking
many are called
but few are seeking
These demons get into them people

Trying to destroy me
Ever since inception
I've noticed the deception
The eternal struggle
Lucifer and Michael
Casted out from heaven
Now I'm living righteousness
Done with the wickedness
These demons won't prevail

Struggling and screaming
It's like tug of war
Between what's right and wrong
Can't go off emotions
I must be strong
there's got to be something bigger
Spirits keep blocking me
stoping me
wont let me move forth
I gotta go back
and regroup
....

(5) Persecution

Looking out the window
they couldn't even leave
all they could do is fight back and grieve
you wouldn't even believe
what they went through
they busted their heads
wanted them dead

but God is the only one who gave them help
God, no one else
he heard their prayers
felt their pain
heard their cries

gangbanging christians
they can't find you
walking through the hood
you're no good
but I can't find you
what you sowed you're reeping it
you shoulda listened to Jesus
woe to you hypocrites and leeches
now you're gone
lost in wickedness iniquity
you gotta pay for what you did to me
there's no escape
terrorized our family
abused my brother
attacked my mother
harrassed my sisters
they all teamed up
busted our windows
spread rumors
to destroy us
but God was watching you all along
wicked christians
persecuted me and my family
because we were muslims
you blame it on the other man
but its the brother man
who persecuted us

for that the LORD will have no remorse for you
for what you did to us
now you're locked up
or bloody dead in the street
the meek did inherent the land
can't you see
what didn't kill me
has made me stronger
persecution
you need enemies
to become better

looking for assylum
none of our neighbors helped
our only refuge
was 112th
us against the neighboorhood
that's how the God ordained it
me and my siblings are all grown up
and we maintained it
the meek did inherent the land
I can proclaim it
this is called persecution
but God gave us retribution
everyday we had to figjht
all day and all night
living hell manifested
tried and tested
God Blessed it

I'm sorry in the 90's
I wasn't about Black revolution
my family was too busy suffering persecution

by these gangbanging christians
surrounded everywhere
not a friend in sight
we had two choices
hide in the house or fight
backstabbing, betrayals
who can you trust
them or us
By the grace of God
we beat the odds
He destroyed those mobs
against one family 200 deep
but the LORD stood by our side
sit back and weep
busted our windows out everyday
all of you will pay someday
the ones that are still alive
but the rest of you didn't survive
shook the dice and played with life
crapped out
and took that ride
on the other side
in a lake of fire
1000 years of torment
day and night

....

(6) Depression

everyone abandoned me
lied on me
wanted to kill me

I wanted suicied
I wanted death
there was nothing left
no hope
no faith
I couldn't smile
I felt dead inside
I used to dream
wanted to be somebody
wanted to study astronomy
but due to the economy
nobody gave me anything
I tried to avoid the streets
buried in a shallow Grave
I craved death
God pulled me out
a reason to live
....

(7) No

I don't want to get involved
I'm not getting sent off
you want it done so do it yourself
we're all men
you don't need my help
I have a future to think about
when you're on top
I was left out
you can't ruin my plans
don't use me to do your dirt

I understand
when I'm locked up
carrying your weight
you wont send me a dime
25 years of wasted time
too many are locked up
sent off by people like you
its messed-up
are your lies and promises
are dressed-up
if you can't do the time
don't do the crime
get out my face
you're wasting time
I don't want your money
don't want your cars
what good are they
when you're behind bars?

Pimpo, you're too simple
get a dose of this info
you're not diligent
you're too ignorant
let it inside of your temple
sell your own dope
no ride on your own foes
no joke suppose those
who chose their own doom
too soon to assume gloom
KABOOM!
he crossed them goons
he froze, he's disapproved
dropped out, shoulda stayed in school

too bad he lost his life
sent off and he paid the price

Forecast gloomy
blocks still booming
stocks still falling
life's still going
streets still talking
creeps still stalking
should've said no
would've still been walking

....

(8) Money was a Stranger

I used to stand outside all day
just to get a glimpse
ever since I was three years old
we've been hustling and struggling
stealing out the store
helping with groceries
pumping gas, collecting cans
but money never came to me
that's why I'm mad
couldn't afford gym shoes
couldn't buy a shirt
wanted to study martial arts
the feeling hurts
until I earned it
no one ever gave to me
is it really worth it
to do crime, to do dirt

just to get a taste
in the end
is it really worth anything with a case
money will leave you six-feet-deep
cold and dry

As a child
I wanted to study astronomy
but due to the economy
money was a stranger to me
I didn't know her
I looked around for her
but couldn't find her
had to work hard just to see her
for a short while
grew up broke
she left me alone because I didn't sell dope
when I did wrong
she came to me quick
in droves
but didn't stick around too long
I didn't grow up expecting her
I didn't depend on her
now that I'm a man
I still don't value her
appreciate or expect anything from her
she's a gold digging floozy
no loyalty
associating with anybody
she caused many men to die
to kill and to go to prison
money has been no friend to me
every time I got her

they always took her away from me
I don't know how to treat her
the only time she stay around
is when I use my mind
and take my time
with faith in abound
Solomon told me
wisdom is more precious than fine gold
understanding than choice silver
money isn't the thing for me
do I really need her?

....

(9) Lookin' For Love

Yesterday was my birthday
but I spent it the worst way
Stuck between a rock & a hard place
I was thinking I wasn't good enough
vernacular ain't hood enough
spent my time and money
but it wasn't good enough
the girl used me
psychologically abused me
she left me for somebody else
she said: she only mess with top notch men
who roll in Cadillacs and Benz
on 22 inch rims
but we can be friends
when I saw her get in
my heart sunk right in
I know what he told her

when that Cadillac rolled up
he made you feel special
in ten minutes he met you
said we can go far
if you get in my car
sold her a dream
and promised the world
equipped with diamonds and pearls
now she's up in his stead
givin' love in his bed
then he dropped her off
and he never called
she's looking stupid messed-up
dream deferred
because the lie was dressed-up
she was lookin' for love.....
she almost taste it
different men, different cars, different faces
she chased it
now she gotta face it
what she had at first was good
but she waste it

Her friends told her
there's more fish in the sea
she can find better than me
and live lavishly
she need a baller
so she can live for free
and have everything
that she couldn't from me
I tried to call her
she wouldn't listen to me

didn't want nothing from me
he can do it better than me
now she's scratchin' and itchin'
she don't realize what's happenin'
that dude gave her the business
I'm not smiling or laughing
I'm talkin' about STDs
I'm talkin' about HPV
and those DVDs
when she came back to me
I told her I'm sorry
I don't mess with those floozies
hoodrats, skizanks and loosies
kept lookin' like Lucy and Vicky
She wanted to be like Nikki
You reeped it now sow it up
wanted to drink it now pour it up
this is life that you're playing with
and I had enough...
we suffered pain for it
I stayed true to the game for it
they got a name for it
I was lookin' for love.....
I almost taste it
let you in to discover my secret places
you erased it
now I must replace it
realities of life
we gotta face it

She said: Don't buy the cow
Get the milk for free
in a couple years

Marwan Fateen

21

you'll be just like me
no family, or friends
my reality
baby mommas the drama
you don't know who's the daddy
one night stands
if only I can do it again
don't look for birds in the bushes
if there's one in your hands
I thought the grass was greener
but its not
Don't give them all that you got
they will use you
your precious priceless goods
they will abuse you
without commitment
your mind is your benefit
people come and they go
but do they benefit
I don't think so
stop lookin' for love...
but I'm open-minded
I know love exists somewhere
we just have to find it

....

(10) The Void

Trying to find what we once had
its lost
felt good but it didn't last
its gone

but you don't give up
it hurts
its long gone
she moved on
she has a new man now
so carry on
territory inhabited
because you abandoned it
your trash
his treasure
now live with it
don't make the same mistakes twice
too many instances
no one can make you happy
its a void
an illusion when you look outside
look within
for fulfillment
true love and appreciation
then you be able to give it
and receive it
until then
you'll be miserable and paranoid
looking for someone else
to fill that void
....

(11) I'm Sorry

I push, I pull back
hang up then call back
how can I hurt you

leave you desert you
I didn't mean to hurt you
I'm sorry

When you were weak
I should have been strength
I'm sorry
When you were weak
I should have been strength
I'm sorry

....

(12) Pain

I can't eat, I can't sleep
been feeling like this for weeks
gave her all that I had
why did she choose me
then mentally abuse me
used me up
when I had her
I didn't want her
now she's gone
someone else has her
is she wrong
its been too long
I must be strong
I must move on
all this pain I have
deep inside
dug my soul
took my heart

used it to bowl
knocked down ten pins
messed with ten men
ten friends
throwing babies out with bath water
relationships

My soul is frozen
Can someone help me
I feel empty
I need melting
....

(13) Alone

Moving at the speed of life
have patience
they say because I don't have a job
I'm nothing
because I believe in myself
they don't want me
they all left me
stuck strugglin'
left hustlin'
trying to get my dreams accomplished
on my own
the origins must be your own soul
bring it out...
the journey to the truth starts right here
our own actions is the proof
no room for fear
come here sister

can I have a moment of time
to shine some of this light
to resurrect your mind
leave the past behind
we have a future to think about
today is built on the past
but tomorrow is what we're about
it starts with today
time to make a change
the way we live, think and behave
no longer conducting ourselves
like we're in a shallow grave
they don't want to see us change
so we can remain slaves
let this light conquer the darkness
so our future will be saved
death dealers in darkness
trying to get a name
prostitutes are shameless
waiting to get fame
its hard to maintain
when nothing really change
twenty years later
things are still the same
cold winters are heartless
we must remain sane

....

(14) Cold Rain

Cold Rain
Its so hard to maintain

I can't take this pain

mentally marinated
spiritually subjugated
emotionally amputated
physically segregated
its on a need to know basis
first you need to know basics
everything has its time and season
lyrics, rhyme and reason
knowing better, showing better
look at the citizens
your brethren
don't change the formula in mid-stream
these are things that make up the kings
she used to dream
but fell for anything
my people are mentally-paralyzed
they don't produce anything
perpetual peasantry
perpetual student
impotent mentality
this is for the prudent
read 28 Deuteronomy
emperors of Sodomy
look at the economy
social dichotomy
you need a spiritual lobotomy
the beginnings of wisdom
is the fear of God's wrath
take a mental, moral and spiritual bath
because the LORD our God
will have the last laugh

cold rain
its so hard to maintain
I can't take this pain
its a strain on my brain
because of God Almighty
I remain
cold rain

....

(15) the smoke will be inhaled

burned
yearned
its not my concern if you failed to learn
you've been warned
its my turn
the smoke will be burned
the residue of death
psychological theft
the leafs of hell
it wont prevail
can't you tell
no matter what we do
the smoke will be inhaled

when the smoke clears
empty fears
empathetic tears
pathetic peers
estranged for years
rearranged

daddies disappeared
while the enemy cheers
I'm like an empty can of beer

the smoke of nature
when demons are captured
controlled by this rapture
in the here after

Every night
I end up in the same apartment
Empty
Alone
Wishing I had someone
To hold in my arms
To spend time with
Is pain and misery my destiny
Will it haunt me forever
Will I ever find true love
Someone with me
To help me
Together

(15b) Black holes

Some of these women
Are like black holes
Sucking everything in
Including your soul
They're out of control
Vampires for a price
You have to pay for them
To evaporate your life

To suck you dry
They're like trolls
A fist with ten fingers
A foot with ten toes
Don't know which way to go
Lost
Confusion
Society's institution
Turning tricks
Prostitution
That's not the solution
Temporary economic satisfaction
The subtraction of the soul
A chemical reaction you can't control
Its like a railroad with no tracks
Egg shells without cracks
The point of no return
Can't come back

Black holes
The legion of doom
Rent them a room
You'll find out soon
Your majesty
Your highness
I don't want you to get mad at me
But your mind is
in an empirical tragedy
A travesty
Its gonna take a miracle
to get you out of this predicament

They're digging for gold

In a sewer without a shovel
The hustle
Lips and thighs
Hips and lies
The truth disguised
You'll get your prize
Don't be surprised
The consolation
These black holes
Will leave your mind froze
Your heart cold
They snatched my soul
And took it to bowl
When did the black women
Become black holes

....

(16) Balance

life is a disagreement
between good and bad
happy and sad
yin and yang
peasants and kings
life is a problem
I am the solution
Darkness and light
pleasure and pain
loss and gain
hot and cold
young and old
scared and bold

Balance
men and women
parents and children
taking and giving
Balance

....

(17) The love of money

You need a Bently to achieve her
This ain't Leave It To Beaver
But the weave and wife beater are cheaper
She's living large off the iphone,
the beeper
They turn their bodies into commodities
Oddities on an odyssey
Your majesty
Your mind is in tragedy
A travesty
Everybody has a price
Anyone can take a life
They're like savages
Conducting themselves
Like low-minded beasts
why?
For the pie in the sky
The pie between the thighs
for the dressed-up lie
Not the best up high

Common creed and philosophy
Captured me into this abyss

Everything is good
Satan's philosophy
A misconception
Devious deception
When you associate success with foolery
Ignorance with jewelry
I associate money with hard work

Money should be utilized
To alleviate the pain
of the psychologically brutalized

They're detrimental to society
ruthless men
Toothless in the pen
Thugs
Known for pushing drugs
Shooting slugs
Where I'm from
We don't trust people with smiles
The greasy
Only for a while
He slipped up
Fell off, the monkey
A junkie
Somebody's flunky

It's a shame
What they'll do for some money
Baby daddy dead
Or in prison
Instead of mourning
Or showing concern

She's with the next man
Waiting for his turn

Thomas Jefferson is still the master
The leader
The redeemer
You're a dreamer
Oh, a diva
Controlled by the devil
Enrolled for forever
Until you get it together
Your cold shoulder
Is worse than the weather

I don't think we can make it
You're mentally buck-naked
It's too tough for you
You can't take it
Your spirit must awaken
Don't get it mistaken
For getting drunk and high
you're too drunk off lies
Kiss your future goodbye
If that's what you need
To get by
....

(18) Larenzo

what's that sound?
I looked up
It was Larenzo

he was flexing that Benzo
I was playing Nintendo
they was playing pretendo
blowing indo
out the window
26 inch wrenches
not to mention
elevated suspension
his bank roll's dented
demented
gets the wenches
can you believe this
perceive this
this dude he achieved this
you can't dismiss this
who is this
be the witness
high school he ditched it
for business
hood riches
his enemies endless
the snitches
found in ditches
let me mind my own buisiness

they took all his cars
and all his cash
he's left on his back
with nothing

Dude came up ballin'
Peep
Then came up missin'

Weep
Then learned his lesson
Deep
All his people left him
Creeps

This fool is locked up
without a nickel to his name
and you're claiming his gang?
madness
Sun Tzu said if a nation take a fall
it can never rise again
sadness
Humpty Dumpty sat on a wall
and split his wig
because he rose too high
and grew too big
silence....

....

(19) Socially absurd

Because he made more money
Got more fame
A bigger name
He must be a better man
But what about the grind
Countless hours of time
On the city streets
Cold winters full of heat
Can't catch a beat
Or break

Outside those camera lights
Might not have money
But I know I'm right
Without you
I keep up the fight
But all you wanted
Was camera lights
And a good night

If you go to my facebook page
I don't have many friends
Does that make him a better man
I don't overstand,
I understand
That means I'm grass roots
Understand
....

(20) The box

Your mind is a prison
Designated to 6 x 9 dimensions
A cell
For the brain
A brain cell
Full of misery and pain
Ignorance, darkness
But you maintain
Stuck in society's ways
You behave
Because to misbehave
Is to step outside

The box

....

(21) Beast

liquor stores in the ghetto
exploiting our women
Foreign oppressors
that's why you're being destroyed
in the east
you got the characteristics of the beast
overseas you're the least
In the eyes of the Almighty, you're a beast
infadel, hypocrite
robbing the poor
usery
selling swine and wine
selling my people pork and spoiled meat
you'll taste the heat
because God don't like ugly
you're making our money
exploiting our women, prostitution
wicked ways
just because you getting paid
don't make it okay
go back to the east
wicked beast
and take all your poison back home
and lease us alone
instead of demonstrating the beast
you're showing us the least
dirty bearded stinking wicked man

in the mother land
made merchandise of the brother man
....

(22) Ad Doho

Gangbanging until eternity
when is it gonna stop?
ending up in infirmaries
dead on the block
institutionalized mischief
scrutinized misfits
perpetual ignorance makes me sick
I'm not a valued member of my race
they only value them members
who's living a disgrace
not brothers with degrees
with high expected dreams
Standing on their creed
providing for their needs
they honor niggas with disease
who strive for Mickey D's
who threw away their lives
chasing government cheese
In the 80's and 90's
they used to hide behind the gang chiefs
but God destroyed the gang chiefs
for their wickedness indeed
Now instead of on their two feet
They're living on their knees
Not a weapon you can conjure
Will prosper against me

It's easy to move on two dudes
When you're walking around ten deep
All for one, one for all
but God don't honor the cowards
devoured all your power
this land will be ours
knocked down the towers
the beast loosing his powers
toss down the flowers
this world soon will be ours

Artificial insemination
Injected into our minds
Chased behind Dr. King's dream
And got left behind
Now we're on these suicidal missions
'til they send those depositions
all that's left is thugs, drugs, killin'
brothers filling in prison
lost, in another dimension
call it eternal detention
sit back and listen
to this exposition, intervention
society's controlling the women and children
they think its independence
slut tactics and rap music
influence and distribution

if you never understood
why you never seen no good
this is the hood
controlled by Hollywood
in the planet of the apes

there's no real escape
this is our fate
but its never too late

Superfly, Foxy Brown
Menace II Society, Neno Brown
Tony Montana sitting on cloud nine
Set It Off and you did those crimes
do your time don't sit back and whine
lost our minds now we're deaf, dumb and blind
……..
we had too much rope
sold too much dope
fell for the okedoke
now we're stuck in this choke hold
they're hustling our vote
the president to the pope
the people and the folks
the beast got 'em in a scope
society's spreading fear
we're stuck in this atmosphere
the people wont care
about nothing
if they're not aware
....

(23) The Serpent

I keep my enemies close
I see your plots and schemes
you want to steal my dreams
so I let you close

to study your antics
degenerate tactics
so I can recognize game
and develop protection
in the future
for the rest of my life
so I fall back
scientifically oberving you
watch those people you call your friends
they smile in your face
but do pretend
their motivaion
their lies and manipulation
tongue play
discrepencies
in everything they say
bottom feeding
chasing leftovers
its ok

You befriended me
You pretended to be a friend of me
But I found out you're the enemy
....

(24) FEAR

We all have it
you just have to manage it
coach it
False Evidence Appearing Real
Conquering fear

Its like fighting a lion
or a bear
Don't panic
The enemy
the unknown
mind control tactics
relax
calm down
take control
take a breath
relax your mind
ease the load
look fate in the eyes
then go home

To be scared is to be dead
Because fear comes from ignorance
And ignorance is darkness
And darkness is death
Face your fears
Or be enslaved to your fear
....

(25) Choice

Today the sun didn't rise
I had a choice
to save my life
life or death
change or stay the same

The black mind is corrupted and crippled

blooded and cripped
decreped and degraded
uncivilized savages
in violation of sacred creeds
our philosophy
drug dealers and shooters
all we want to be
animalistic mindset
sick thoughts
we have an addiction to being a victim
do a root cause analysis
to find out the solution

....

(26) A victim of time

I retreat to this solitude
This attitude
Like empty faucets when you're thirsty
My resistence is my only weapon
I'm tired of living for nothing
It's time to live for something
Taking my life into my own hands
To be a man
It's time to die for something
Give life and try for something

Take this, take that
Regret
And to the dreams
Depressed
No fighting God

Your best bet is to humble yourself
Waiting, procrastinating
Tired of existence
Scared to make a difference
To succeed
Proclaim your disbelief
They're on the front porch
Waiting to die
Waiting on their mommas to cry
Looked up
Time passsed them by
Doing nothing
The difference between lyrics and life
We are shadows of time
Tomorrow you can be gone
One hour, one minute
Only for a moment
Then gone
All we have in this world
Is one day
It's a foregone conclusion
What's the solution
You only live once
That's your excuses

It's hard making it alone
That's why so many people
End up selling their souls
To secret societies
Masons and Greeks
People and Folks
You people are weak
Stand on your own two feet

Be a man
God will send his angels
To chop you down

No opportunities
Couldn't find me a job
Holes in my shoes
I had to go to school
Hand-me-down clothes
Can't be no fool

We're set up to fail
By design
No even playing field
We're wasting time

I can make it out here alone
Some of us don't have a choice
Stand right here and sing your song
But some of us don't have a voice
....

(27) A Place

I need a place to call my own
a place to call my home
a place I could to run to
introduce my son to
Its amazing
extraordinary
its called peace of mind
you can have a piece of mine

I don't love money
I love life
Life is wisdom
Without a price
Both from the streets
And from college
I'm a philosopher
The love of knowledge

I broke out those chains
Consciousness
Enslaved to my ideology
My beliefs
There is a state of mind
Called kind
which we all can inhabit
A place once known to us all

Deep inside my mind
is blind
Pain inside
must leave behind

When we die
All of our material possessions,
including our bodies
Will be left behind
....

\\\\\/////

Part Two

The Enlightenment

(28) The Flesh

I woke up yearning
this feeling keeps calling
my mind keeps stalling
it keeps me from falling
for the flesh
the spirit knows best
there's bigger things in this world
than the flesh
bottom line
I got things to do in the morning
I can't keep going everytime the flesh pulls me
no more time
recognize this
everything you do revolves around the flesh
you work all week
to provide for the flesh
held hostage
captivity, slavery
too many excuses
you're useless
save me
justify pushin' poison
to feed your flesh
food, clothes and shelter
to please the flesh
revolutionary struggles
to free the flesh
not for God, the mind or soul
just the flesh
and you're the best
needing your oppressor to feed your flesh...

The original flesh
oh, the original man
you do what you can
but don't understand
that there's more to a man than just the flesh
you're a pest
beggiing just to feed your flesh
if you give a man a fish
he eats for a day
but if teach him to fish
he eats forever
then there's more than the flesh
that keeps things together

The flesh doesn't want you
the flesh doesn't need you
if the flesh could, the flesh would eat you
defeat you
mistreat you
it's evil
what profit the flesh
when your mind is still miserable
hair and nails
shoes and clothes
getting your flesh dressed-up
neglecting your soul
judging me because of my flesh
no, because of my skin
I occupy this flesh
but I wont pretend
the flesh is a tool
to be used
to create and maintain

Parts of Man: The Declaration of Truth

and to occupy the fools
in the physical realm
there is no rules
to achieve the flesh
you gots to believe the flesh
its a test
the good side and bad side
of the flesh
pleasure and pain
there's a dark side to the flesh
disease
a moment of silence
to grieve
you starve the soul
but the flesh is your nucleus

spiritual castration
you need a vacation
it's a condition
psychological deviation
it deceives the flesh
don't believe the flesh
you must resist the temptation
spiritual deprivation
mental frustration
the flesh calls the shots for you
manipulation
predatory savages
low-minded beasts
40 year old men plotting to feast
using their tongue to seduce the chicks
to disease their flesh
reproducing yourself

filthy scum
I detest
They say the good die young
well then the wicked become old men
What am I?
Am I the lust that makes up the flesh
....

(29) Image

Identity
you're idea of self
bleaching and creaming
to become someone else
wasting billions
do you see the maddness?
want happiness, I see sadness
blame society, I blame culture
swoop down grabbing their minds
like a vulture
feeding on their heads
the mentally dead
it contaminates the mind
untold effects it cause to the brain
we all know what it does to the culture
collective attitudes.
ideas and expectations
our collective vision
its self-destruction
leads to exploitation
and manipulation
our self-esteem is too low for us to care

due to the fact
that we want someone else's hair
until we care or have self worth
ever since birth
no one taught you self worth
self-respect, self-love
they always told you
you're not good enough
so you perm your hair
bleach your skin
and chase thugs
because that's the only time in life
you gets loved

you want to be thugs
and sell them drugs
encouraged by society
because you think you're not good enough
demeanar ain't hood enough
so you imitate plastic thugs on TV
if not you look at the ones down the street
money, cars, women
everything you need
until you end up
lying dead in the street
or in jail
but you don't care
self-fulfilling prophecy
you don't study
you ditch school
too busy chasing the image
to look cool
to get the money, to get the cars,

then the girls
you don't wanna learn because no one
respects a square
but you'll learn as soon
as you're life's a nightmare
can't leave the house
can't go to school
can't take a walk
the other plastic thugs want your life
what you got
for street cred, for fame, for the girls
the same things you wanted in life
from the world
polyester, manufactured, man-made
not self-created, originated, God-made

All around the world
they suffer from self hate
skin bleaching
looking like paste
it's a discrace
erased your face from society
don't get mad at me
it's reality
skin tanning
I don't understand it
they say image is everything
integrity is nothing
its time to be redefined
and live for something
take pride in yourself
stop hiding yourself
be happy for who you are

not somebody else

....

(30) Cultural Slave

Because you're in western civilizaion
you think you're free
but you're a slave to the culture
subjected to someone else's behavior
someone else's style
someone else's ideas
you're gone wild
we are spiritual beings
an individual
when you take on those thoughts
you're not individual
a replication
a duplication
society's imagination
a slave to the music
you're following the leader
peer pressure
not that voice deep inside
what about your thoughts
your ideas about life
that you hide
you coincide
replace them with someone else's thoughts
transplanted them into your mind
thats your fault
you volunteer, participate, you behave
partly because you're afraid

that alone is what makes you a slave
all around America
they're embracing the same thoughts
they dress, they act
they look like everyone else
who's an individual
capable of embracing and demonstrating
their own thoughts?
scared to think your thoughts,
be yourself, you're afraid
this is the land of the free
home of the brave
but its also the land of the cultural slave

Assimilate, emulate
simulate
stimulate, participate
its too late
hypnotize chant your spell create hell
still locked up in them jail cells
braggin'
60 years old and your pants still saggin'
now you're runnin' around with tight pants
mohawks and tight fades
you might as well live in a cave
if you allow society mainstream culture
to dictate how you behave
you're nothin' but a slave
"from the cradle to the grave"
....

(31) The Watchman

A thousand pardons
may I speak to you this day
I have a few issues
I'd like to address to you
today
is it ok
may I say
is it a good day
its been getting ignored way too long
for us to wait
the sheep's been left way too long
and has gone astray
the enemy has grown way too strong
so we can't delay
you have my sincere apologies
if you get offended
but this subject matter is way too real
for me to pretend it

"Woe to the shepherds"
for leading the sheep astray

Preachers and pastors
the congregation is your sheep
Nicolaitaine Doctrine
using the blood of Jesus
Excusing your wickedness
spiritual prostitution
Gang leaders and rappers are shepards
Woe to you too

you influence the culture
their blood is upon you
teachers
the students are your sheep
the mass public is your sheep
Mother's and fathers
children are you sheep
you wonder why they're messed-up
misguided, misled
unfed
but you claim you're doing big
independent women
look what you did
what you're producing
mental, spiritual, physical pollution
distribution
you judge a tree by the fruit it produces
wicked fruit
the children of thugs
you blame society
I blame you
contaminated with your evil ways
"THUG LIFE
The Hate U Gave"
all their life
shouldn't have bred with wickedness
children of sin
falling for that anything
low life men
spiritual leaders
look at the damage its causing
read the book of Revelations
Nicolaitaine Doctrine

Jesus Said he hated it
but you're preaching it
leading the blind to the bottomless pit
to the slaughter
woe to you wicked shepherds
taking advantage
getting fat off their ignorance
drunk off your lies
using grace
its a disgrace
a disguise
its a trickle down effect
society will be next
following your waste
Building temples for the sluts and sodomites
Its all about the money
Excusing lascivousness
Justifying your wickedness
you preachers are hypocrites
Poverty pimps in pool pits
the people perish
because of your vision

Strip joints and abortion clinics
the sheep are deaf, dumb and blind
they follow anything
they stand for nothing
and fall for anything
in their mind
the shepherds can do no wrong
they're always right
they're the leaders
they clothe, shelter and feed them

mentally, physically and spiritually
culturally you're satisfied
in all aspects of life
the flesh, death, wickedness and strife
you love what you do
because the shepherds say it's right
you love where you are
because you think you're going far
wait a minute
it gets deep.
the pit gets deep
narrow and steep
blind are the sheep
the watchman over the sheep
must warn them

....

(32) The World

They're murdering millions
in the name of Democracy
spreading hypocracy
blaming Khadafi
look at your own country
corporate slavery
sugar-coating reality
elitist pranks
corporate banks sank
do you think presidents are kings?
allocating our money
to give to the thieves
corporate greed

it's in their genes
its a trickle-down effect
from the peasants to the kings

Your education is useless
if all it produces
is cup-holding constituents
prostitution candidates
gun-toting residents
savages
it's evident
that what you learned is irrelevant
if it's all about the cash
until you're left on your a#$
with no back-up plan
if the money didn't last

Fallacious philosophies
enslaved to identities
corrupting the youth
twisting the truth
influencing their mentality
the wrong way
encouraging criminality
or become gay

Ethical pollution
hoodrats and homothugs
prostitution and selling drugs
at home you show no love
outside they're shooting slugs

People are having children for no reason

they grow up and go to prison
daddy didn't want a son
he wanted flesh
momma didn't want a child
she want a check
what about the future
the next hundred years
will we even be here?

The evolution of thought
headed one way
the revolutions are fought
to bring a better day
the constitutions are brought
because the children are taught
being righteous is God's way
the institutions are sought
so the leaders are bought
to maintain society
the status quo
class strugglin'
drug smugglin
media disguising it
you're not realizing it
for 200 years
we cried 200 tears
we're still here, ignorant
back to Africa on slave ships
the price of life
if you can't afford it
don't try to distort it
they wont report it
....

(33) The Determinator

Society wants me to be dependent
on a people
they allegedly had us in captivity
Slavery
Emancipation proclamation
The occupation of my mind and soul
But I want control of my destiny
Self determination
Duediligence
Its like finding out there's no Santa Claus
At five years old
Where do we get those toys
Reality
Society
Life is too cold
For fantasy
I call that insanity
A disgrace to humanity
The only thing you think
You can do with knowledge
Is serve the white man

They told me
The white man was our oppressor
Now they tell me
I'm lesser
Because he's not my master
Work a job
Kunta Kente to Rodney King
Can't we all just get along

forget dignity
and being a man
and taking your destiny into your own hands
just get a job from the white man
and hold his hand
I'm tired of asking the white man
For everything
Who is he
I'm tired of expecting the white man
To do everything
What about me
He's not my father
nor my god
Everything he can do
I can do it better
Clever
Forever

....

(34) Ignorance Equality

In an equal state of darkness
we're all born
each day is opportunity
to escape

to a higher level
we elevate
we must appreciate
struggling, suffering
separate

we must achieve the light
what's wrong aint right
don't deceive the night
or defeat the fight

you must get to the light
but you're stuck in the dark
every night

with the same amount of ignorance
we begin
in the same amount of darkness
everyone is
equality, equalibrium
the continuum

the key factor in our dimension
the one thing
we all have in common
is ignorace
we attend school
to ensure prosperity
alleviate poverty and distress
because ignorance and responsibility
don't mix
....

(35) Reading

its like digging thru rocks and dirt
To get to the treasure
You need the map

The road block
Location
And plot a course
Treasures buried in this world
Just gotta find them
Appreciate the struggle
You dug thru the dirt
This treasure
Understanding
Worth
You go through a lot of dirt
To get to the gold
Don't confuse the two
used to put us on trees
for trying to read
now you're avoiding it
like its a disease
....

(36) Revolutionary Pimp

Manipulate and manuever the mind
false teaching
for your own economic gain
socialist marxist
capitalizing off the people's pain
its a shame
went from crook dreams
to book schemes
anything to get fame
a righteous name
so they'll trust you with everything

pyramid schemes up in Egypt
all this stuff about oppression
but you're the one doing the oppressing
perpetually struggling
sarcastically speaking
I'ma connect the truth
this is the proof
you can't dilute

Abulance chasing reactionary simp
too impatient
revolutionary pimp
went from Mumia to Troy Davis
Lord please save us
the people wont praise
our shiesty lude behavior
capitalizing off any situation
running back and forth
with no consistent destination
looking for anything the other man
did to the brother man
so we can protest and complain
for cheap fame
not a thing changed
but your name
skyrocketed to public fame
it's a shame
poverty pimps
by no other name
....

(37) Falsehood

Fallacious philosophies
based on mythologies
they're attacking the mind, soul and body
in wicked nefarious ways
false history
false doctrine
false disease
false treatment
to give your civilization a treatment
under the pavement
obiliterated from reality
the Judas goat
Benedict Arnald
producing a dead man
digging his own grave
that he praise
the more he learn
the more he burn
you let them
give you false history
running back to Africa
where's the slave ships
the plantations
all I see his movies
imagination
where's the evidence
where's the proof
where's the truth
my people weren't in captivity
what about you?
the dressed-up lie

everything that looks and sounds good
isn't necessarily right

Identity crisis
you're trying to find it
you can't get back Egypt
the wilderness
just look behind it
you'll find everything you used to know
throughout the ages
even if you can
you won't understand
their ancient practices
customes and ways
best to focus on today
the void is too deep to fill
when you're focused on the wrong places
yesterday isn't necessarily relevent today
take those concepts, ideas and scriptures
adapt and apply them today
its the only way
my people are lead astray

There is no such thing as HIV
Magic Johnson, Easy E
Eunice Rivers in Tuskeegee
lying about bad blood
now its bad disease
who ever seen it?
in 25 years, they never isolated it
in lamens terms
they never found it
in a human being

how do they test it?
deductive reasoning
the body produces antibodies
to fight disease
if it reacts to antigens
on a swab
therefore you have HIV
what they don't tell us is
antibodies react to anything
modern tuskeegee
a social construct
it don't exist in reality
but we believe anything
due to the fact that
they're the authorities
do what you're told
take toxic drugs
and keep your mouth shut
had enough

No one will believe in you
if you don't believe in yourself
people love, people hate
protesting fate
where nothing is real
you can spend a $3 bill
there's only one universal truth
in the physical real
there's infinite paths to get there
which creates diversity
humanities greatest asset is the mind

(37b) The Attack on Sambo
its time to go Rambo
taking no prisoners
payment for what you're doing to us
Mr. Charlie
Mr. Slave
buck dance on T.V.
why did you let the corporation enslave you
nothing you can say right now
will save you
its too late
now meet your fate
there's no escape
this double-edged sword
will chop your soul
and your face
Arnold Swartzinegger
I'm terminating these sambos
....

(38) Stolen Legacy

Infamous warriors
erased from history
do we know anything
Trail of tears
but we scream abuot slavery
its a mystery
but what about my story
the war of 1812
Black history

African American
do you know what it is
let's define it
but stay reminded
the difference between race and nationality
its reality
Society is stealing my legacy
breading with us to steal our identity
....

(39) Token Black

We live in reality
but you don't know why
token Black
you never spoken back
on the slave plantations
you took the pain
held back
didn't try to fight back
they call you token Black
the only Black in the enviornment
from birth to retirement
uncle tom
Sambo
Kunta Kente
tryna be something you ain't
walk the plank
....

(40) They Feast

they feast off foolery
they feast off ignorance
indulge in stupity
in darkness
they feast off the least
they feast with the beast
trying to be cool
rotten teeth
they feast
....

(41) Guilt

you can't stand to bear the shame
you can't deal with it
your fathers stole our land
chill with it
take responsilility
stop sweaping it under the rug
you polluted our people with drugs
turn our women into independent sluts
destroyed our homes
denied our rights
in all your wars
we're made to fight
to defend your rights
while we're denied our own
God don't like wickedness
you'll answer to the lord

just like Rome
the truth hurts
it comes from knowing you're wrong
you caused that harm
you try to be good
but it burns your soul
....

(42) The Soul

I came up with something
let me share it with you
Everyone wants to be loved
and everything we do
Good or bad
is to satisfy our desire for love
our lust
our need
to be recognized
to be achieved
to be appreciated
for attention
It starts with a voice to a vision
from a vision to creation
invention
intention
without a voice
there is no choice
they're detached from reality
through ignorance

they dropped bombs and planes

on us
they ran scams and games
on us
they sold hopes and dreams
to us
they hung ropes and names
to us

This pitiful propaganda
Being waged against us
Unfair
Unjust
But we put our faith and trust
in lies and rumors
without proof
Psychologically stepped on
Thats why I left home
If they knew better
They would do better

I forgot about the rain
then it came
if this wasn't enough
can you take this pain
and maintain
my mind
these rhymes
complain to your own soul
that way no one else will know
it will motivate you to grow
your naked soul
get some clothes
clothe your heart

with clues
I'm confused
the soul
....

(43) Fight

Put your fist to the pavement
stand up
don't give in to enslavement
man up
take life one step at a time
design your plan
your blue print
your guide
it will take time
work at your construction
everyday
your ideas are everything
don't throw them away
keep your mind on your future
25,000 mile journey
step by step
just bcause you're having a hard time right now
see it through
there's greater days ahead
its up to you
our destiny is in our hands
children of men
success or failure only begin
when you give in
you're almost at the finish line

you can win

Tap into your spirit
tap into your thoughts
eternal chanpions
battles to be fought
spiritual, mental, physical
mystical
I dug up your talent
you're no challenge
invincible

....

(44) Dedication

giving all that you have
for the cause
for the art
or just your self
maybe someone else
whatever the case may be
you don't half step
you give your best
100%

....

(45) Self-Determination

I'm in charge of my own destiny
the CEO of my own reality

to be is idealistic
set high standards
and work toward becoming them
I did my dudilligence
this is the evidence
sometimes you gotta go back
in order to move forward
self-actualization is the realization
of who you've always been
you just became
could've recognized then
and remained the same
because the truth don't change

....

(46) Love

I think I found true love
so I'll sing abuot it
I used to dream about it
heard good things about it
its the love for myself
I'm so glad I found it
I can't give you something I don't have
you can't love me if you hate yourself
if you found it
you'd wanna share it
you don't got it
you'd hate to bare it
find it within
before you give it out

....

(47) Beauty

indestructable
it comes from within
it isn't just physical
it doesn't begin or end
what good is skin
when there's nothing inside
nothing mental
nothing spiritual
its not beneficial
a moment of pleasure
nothng real
whats real doesn't die
it last past a minute

beauty is truth
truth is proof
proof is evidence
not neglegence
the beauty of life
creation
....

(48) Dreams

don't run from dreams
or be scared of what you might see
affraid of what they could be
if you dream
dreams are things
themes

schemes
whatever you percieve
what you hope to achieve
believe
used to be
comes back to haunt
your chance to deal with it
and move on
diabolical thoughts
manifested
people thought it was gone
but God test it

We live a spiritual life
every night
and a physical life
everyday
they're interonnected
day and night
you call them dreams
I call them life
take what you realize here
for spiritual development
take what you realize there
for physical evolution
mental perfection
our link to God
God sends his angels in dreams
for our development
....

(49) Reality

tear drops
explosions
opened hands
behold them
mine eyes are opened
40 slaves
I sold them
I see men wasting
their lives on porches
drinking, smoking
thinking about Porsches and bacon
hoping
to have a kingdom
is to be captain of your own dome
a night of pleasure
can't last forever
I see no shame
abomination
2/3 of a man
a perpetual priion
used you to block my vision
The hell you create
Your self-determination
Born in a shallow grave
God pulled me out
We're symbolic beings
The naked soul
The naked truth
We're the same person
In different bodies
Miscegenistic

A tragic misfit
Too simplistic
Elevate the people's mind
A mental morturary
Read the obituary
Deteriorated brain
Psychologically confiscated
The mind is vulnerable
Easily penetrated
Constantatly manipulated
Open other avenues
Escapism
Can't go anywhere you choose
Racism
Desensitized society
No more Caleco Vision and Atari
Grand Theft Auto
Safari
Jacking and robbing
trying to keep up with Santa Claus
My father didn't make enough momey for food
on Christmas Eve
Stomach growling
watching reruns of Different Strokes
....

\\\\\\//////

Part Three

The Renaissance

(50) Mine Eyes

As I sit back
And glance at eternity
I decipher and determine my destiny
This right here
Isn't how things are supposed to be
The spirit gets close to me
I feel it
Let me give you a glimpse
Of what my eyes have seen
They call them windows to the soul
so jump right in
Take a peek into my soul
From outside in
I have bad news
Life is what you make it
No short cuts
Hard work and appreciation
I stand on this mountain
I see doom and destruction
Our son is dying
Angels are crying
Preachers are lying
Rivers overflowing
The blind leading the blinded
But I see the pit
The hole
We're being led to the slaughter
To the cliff
Because of our ignorance, and wickedness
I've seen death coming for me
The Grim Reaper chasing me

Backstabbing, treachery
I saw the hands of God saving me
I see falsehood
Lies and deceit
Fornication, adultery
Men seducing the next man's wife
Selling their souls for such a cheap price
The rat race
The paper chase
For bread crumbs, for sugar gum
Greed and corruption
I see misery coming from your face
Happiness is no kin or friend to you
The fall from grace
I looked up
In the mist of reality
I find myself falling
I see danger
Gloom
Once you were the groom
Now you're getting swept up
With the broom
Banks are robbing the society
Taking our money
Giving it to the wealthy, the greedy
In the bull pen
I saw a man crying
18 years old
They gave him 60 years
He shouldn't have done what he did
The murder
He chose the wrong career
Should've just walked away

Could've became a doctor or lawyer someday
Too bad he threw his life away
Walking right here
You're no better than anyone else
You walk the same steps
You take the same breaths
Your economics and prestige is irrelevant
Walking right here
I see snooty snobs
Lesbians and gays are everywhere
And Glutness blobs
When will man rise
The angel cries
When will man rise
The angel cries
I've fallen and I can't get up
Can you help me
Hell is right next to me
I feel like a curse
Even worse
I feel like I'm cursed
I see a generation lost
Men and women
I see faces
Suffering
The graveyard walking
Society's all messed up
They got us robbing and killing
Selling drugs, prostitution
To quench our thirst
Its open season
Nowhere is safe
Nowhere to hide

They got the whole world
Selling their souls
Chasing this paper
Committing capers
Just for some paper
Pimping our daughters and sisters
As I look up
I see stars falling
Angels calling
God is warning us
From falling into the pit
Blindly
Recognize the signs and seasons
This is the reason
Our loved ones are leaving
We need something to believe in
Money, drugs, cars
Wont save them
When God takes them
He alone creates them
Money lies and fame made them
Pedophile rapist
Stealing innocence from children
The planet is dying
The government is lying
Ignorance is bliss
So we're not trying

....

Parts of Man: The Declaration of Truth

(51) Look at Me

When you look at me
I'm more than the flesh you see
you see a person
but that's not me
I'm what your eyes can't see
I'm the spirit that occupy me
I'm more than me
I want you to get to know who I really am
outside of what your eyes may see
this body is something I use
to navigate this existence
we existed before the body we chose to inhabit
we fall short when we start associating who we are
to the body we dwell
we're all made from darkness
in darkness we dwell

we navigate the ether
we navigate the ether
every night
we navigate the ether
you're going to be the teacher
we need someone to reach her
every night
we navigate the ether

God gives the sun and light
to all those who's wrong or right
equal opportunity
the spirit wants unity
all that really matters

is you and me

....

(52) I'm an Ant

I'm dist-ant
An inhabit-ant
of c-ant
I'm an ant
Part of a larger whole
A body
that we all control
Take away the tee
And you'll find me
Free
I'm not
I can't
Because I'm an ant
Apostrophe
Catastrophe
Stop asking me
Nagging me
I pleases thee
Can't you see
It's a burden on me
I'm to be free
Please set me free
The only one for that
Is me
The ant
That can't

We are the ant
Who's antics are not unique
Antique
Consist-ant
Persist-ant
A domin-ant contest-ant
The opposite of irrelev-ant
Resentment
I need a complement
not a compliment
You are repugn-ant
The embodiment of disgusting
Your antagonistic tactics are obvious
Oblivious
Sycophantic
Frantic
Robotic clones
Get in line
Leave me alone
I'm an ant in this habitat
An inhabit-ant
the ant

....

(53) Words

Things that are eternal
they have truth
derived from the deepest parts of the soul
they have proof
everlasting
to get it without asking

knowledge, wisdom, and understanding
they are powerful things
can be WMDs
or producers of peace
your reality depends on them
they destroy
they rebuild
can save your life
or get you killed
better watch what you say
on these streets
a wise man told me one day
he don't speak
because a fool runs his mouth
without thinking
everything you say out there
will come back to you
they manifest reality
create wealth or poverty
words are magnificent things
they bring everything
they cause everything
words are constructions
fortified structiures
without a solid foundation
to the necleus
they can sink in and fall
navigate them words
in the right direction
they have power
....

(54) Music

Grooving to the tune of life
harmony and peace
frequency the beat
symphony
never overshadowing
neither causing battles
Reduced to a cheap thrill
entertainment
manufactured mentality
falsification of reality
Bitterness
Anger
you're a hoax
Stereotyped
put in a box
characerizaion
just because you got locks
recognize realirty
African, American
subconscious condition
without your awareness
your body reacts to what you hear
you're programmed
without your awareness
metamorphasis
without realizing it
you're comminting genocide
on your own identity
you're like Pavlo's dog
salivating to insanity
....

(55) Royalty & Peasantry
(the choices we make)

You can either rule the world
or mop the floor
depending on your level of knowledge
it seperates peasants from kings
distinguishes crooks and thieves
from chiefs and queens
what do you know
what can you do
are you qualified
if you work in a position
would you come through
Homer Simpson
playing Ini Mini Miny Moe
pressing a botton
you're not qualified to polish shoes
because you dropped out of school
now "I pity you fool"
its bigger than 2 + 2
you blame them
I blame you
due to the fact
that you rejected knowledge
you called them lame
because they went to college
you played the game
got street fame
had all the cars
now you can't get a job
so you blame the world
but you chased the girls

by any means
stealing cars or selling drugs
misdermeanors and felonies
piled up
no one's hiring
no college degree or GED
mentally crippled
the true definiion of a lame
look at your qualificatoins
your only hope is an education
at least enterprise
but without knowledge
that's highly unlikely
its makes the last become first
turns the best into the worst
if the information is too complex for you
then take a course

What separates and distinguishes
the peasants from kings
knowledge, wisdom and understanding
in all aspects of life
it separates man from beast
....

(56) Wisdom

More precious than fine Gold
or diamonds
all the money on Earth can't buy it
the tree of life
through experience and sacrifice

you might find it
everything you lost
a small portion is worth it
your gain
is more than you could have dreamed
imagined
wisdom
in the hands fools is blindness
but in the hands of the wise
is righteous
think twice before doing anything
don't let anger cloud your judgement
psychological adreniline
a mental boost
God will protect the innocent
so I speak the truth
the rest is up to you

A wise man told me one day
if you got hands and brains
you shouldn't be broke
if the government don't represent you
why vote?
its a joke
forty acres, forty mules
gave us a couple dollars
back under the yoke
why smoke?
you got enough problems
sucking on nicotine smoke
wont solve them
everything you reep in this life
you gotta pay the price

don't shake the dice
or take a life
if you can't pay the price
two cups of knowledge
an ocean of wisdom
the only thing in life
that you have
is your wisdom
life is about knowledge
if you're not learning
you're burning
stop turning
life into a wasteland
its a crime

....

(57) New World Order

I establish this decree today
children of men
who's living in iniquity
children of sin
Black Greek
secret scientist
The Black man needs to change
from a savage
reform
elevate
to a better form
outside the norm
quiet storm

a revolution
from society's scorn
reborn
the only solution
its just begun
put down your gun
pick up those books
stupid crooks
givin' dirty looks
in county jails
dirty locks
living hell
to achieve
your dreams
is to believe
I set this decree
violations
will be handed out by God
any questions?

by the power vested in me
I set this decree
that anyone who violates
will answer to God

....

(58) The Truth

A double-edge sword
cutting both ways
without respect for man
without bias, prejudice

it is what it is
objective reality
hate it or love it
but you can't change it
it heals, it hurts
you just gotta except it
its not something to mess with
just respect it
you can't neglect it
reject it
reject yourself
check yourself
before you get wrecked
by yourself

knowledge is like water
drink a cup
wisdom is the life it brings
sustains the Earth
can't get enough
pulled me out my shallow grave
I couldn't get up
the breath of life
I needed help
couldn't do it myself
the LORD sent his angels
to get me out
guided me in the right direction
it was my choice
or stay in the pits of hell
until it was all up

everything your thoughts concieve

what your nostrals breathe
what your eyes believe
you can achieve

The truth is a tree
It stands in the day or the night
It doesn't demish
You chop it down for its substance
It can feed a nation
Produce wealth
Provide health
Climb too high
it Provides death
It keeps growing
The river of life
It keeps flowing
....

(59) Forgiveness

A perpetual prison
used you to block my vision
I don't know who to trust
fake people all the same
looking for someone to blame
I forgive you
I forgive you all
the LORD used you to punish me
I was blind but now I see
I'm on this path
I use this pen
God put it on our hearts

I'm asking you
please forgive me for the wickedness
I did to you

In life you reap what you sow
if its good, we will know
if its not, you will go
somebody's trying to kill me
I don't know who it is
I'm paranoid
I don't trust anybody
all my friends are guilty
they're my enemies
they don't got my back
who I thought were my guys
were really haters and spies
spreading rumors and lies
backstabbing
silly rabbit
tricks are for idiots
drug habbit
you had to have it
who do I trust
God is my only ally
He will deliver me
he will save me from my enemies
....

(60) Corruption

Drunk off power
greed for money

without consequences
decadence
your wickedness shine
you pay no mind
to the truth
the synagogs proof
put your faith in no man
just the truth
what's the use
no checks and balances
no accountability
blind trust from society
a dangerous combination
if there's nothing inside
ethical foundation
moral fabric
your righteousness hide
wickedness collide
and take over
its time for an extreme makeover
God don't like ugly
you'll pay for it
greed
government and corporations taxing
and raping the people
stealing all the money
little to no reciprocity
patronizing
stealing all the property
....

(61) Spiritual Warfare

Who gets to inhabit these bodies
you or me
lets put our faith to the test
and we'll see
you got your click, got your strap, got your mob
I got my faith, got my trust up in God
according to physical science
I'm against the odds
but that's only 2% of reality
the rest is unkown
I have spiritual forces with me
you're left alone
I trust in God
you trust the gun
The LORD bent the bullets from me
jammed your gun
delivered you into my hands
I let you run
but its too late
you sealed your fate
tough Tony
jabroni, without your cronies
you're phony baloney
the wicked shall be destroyed
while the righteous shall survive
this is spiritual selection
the natural part of life
now you're walking around paranoid
looking both ways
but God got it in for you
no escape

But I won't do a thing to you
It's God's hands
he got six million ways to do you in
that's His plan
repent your sins
better change up your ways
before you end up eliminated
from the race
David slew Goliath
how Judah did those Phillistines
no matter how mighty you are
against God you can't do anything

Evolution of the soul
survival of the fittest
God has the hearts of men
understand it
fished me out of the sea
we establshed physical reality
to give the soul a home
to grow and learn
gladiator school
there's wicked forces in the universe
they know no rules
the good gone astray
let us test oursleves
so we'll be equipped on that day
when eternal evil is releassed from the pit
the battle will be for keeps
so lead the sheep
only the fit in spirit
will be complete
its a spiritual war

God needs soldiers
many are called
but few are chosen
the criterion
resist temptation
Satan has already won
from our deviation
the pure in heart
not ruled by flesh
will pass the test
these are the best
Heaven will be established on this Earth
we can rest

....

(62) I'm an Ousider

Outcasted
my soul belongs to the LORD
that's why I'm outside
while you're sitting in
I'm feeding the people truth
while you pretend
I stand to the east
with my back to the beast
you stand to the beast
with your hands in the feast
begging crying on your knees
psychological disease
worshipping his money
can't serve two masters
God and mammon

pathologically lying
all to feed your pockets
let me quench your thirst
the last will be first
the meek will inherent the Earth
you'll realize your worth
and you'll detest your birth
the best is meant for us
....

(63) Being

Because I'm a Black man
I must be a criminal
subliminal
but all I do is exist
people focus too much on doing
when you do
you use your flesh
all you gotta do is be
thats when you use your mind
more than the flesh
the difference between checkers and chess
I feel like and alien
alienated from society
isolated from reality
the only one who understands
the only one who sees the plan
on the planet Earth
mental captivity
prisoner since birth
with these human beings

I'm just a being
being
while you're trying to become
what I AM
chief amongst men
duty and obligation
administration
mental, spiritual, physical exploration
without hesitation
giroscopic energy rotating the object
that's my creation
when you be
you live according to your principles and creed

Woke up this morning
threw on my flesh
triple darkness
triple death
the physical is the last frontier
when there's nothing left
headed to those unknown realms
after death
I manifest
I'm an alien
spiritual flesh
the speed of thought
It wont get caught
or get taught
but its sought
rotate your mind
or get left behind
press rewind
stop throwing pearls to swine

its your time
its a conspiracy
to keep us all in line
connect the dots
and read between the lines

....

(64) the I, the Ing, the Who

I stepped thru this portal of doom
Entereth into the matrix
My mother's womb
It wont be too soon
Looking through these cerebral archives
Pretty soon we will arrive
And have no choice
But to strive and thrive
To survive
When my people were strung out on crack
PCP, heroine, and gang attacks
Back
When Michael Jackson was still Black
Before I hit this planet
I was supposed to be ing
but I chose to become king
The ing is a thing
But a king is over everything
Dominance, dominion
Realm, reality, existence
I just hit this dimension
What is this invention
I find myself trapped in

Flesh, clay
My foundation is dust
My occupation is lust
My only hope is to trust
In the LORD, God
He sent me here
For a purpose
A task
Should I find it out on my own
Or should I just ask?
There's only one person, I
Divided in different bodies
From an ocean to a cloud to a river
To a cup of water
God breathed the breath of life into Adam
From Adam into Eve
The beginning of humanity
To understand the ing
Is to become oneself
Separate from the ing
The body is a thing
The body is the ing
The I is the spirit
I am the mind
The who is the systematic combination
The correlation
Between the I and the ing
The name, personality, identity,
nationality, race and creed
Wicked and good deeds
Point A to point B
Everything in-between
The ing is a person, place or thing

That is, was and will be
Animated in physical existence
It has a beginning and an ending
I exist as the ing
For a moment of time
Two sides
Good and evil
Light and darkness
We're in-between
I am king
You are queen
Unsolved mysteries
About to be revealed
Although you have fallen
Your spirit can be healed
Seven seals revealed
Christ paid our bill
The ing is flesh
A biological thing at best
The ing is a test
Consciousness at rest
The I is the soul
Put to the greatest test
Entrapped in the ing
Escaped to a thing
The eternal struggle
The I against the ing
God against Satan
Spirit against flesh
The I and the ing
Incorporation
Internal investigation
Trying to determine

Parts of Man: The Declaration of Truth

Who you will be
The who has a purpose
The who is temporation
Serve God or serve Satan
I am to be resisted
I am to be existed
Camouflaged by ignorance
My body is the ing
But I am king
The light and the life
Are temporary fabrications
The I is truth
I am proof
Who is the I
Where is the I
What is the I
When is the I
And why is the I
Who is this I
Which everyone claims to be
The answer is quite simple
Me

....

(65) Life

Biological wisdom
They call me human being
They introduced me to violence
Introduced me to hate
Introduced me to silence
This is my fate

Outside the gate
Afraid to walk in

I got two pawns and a rook
I'm trying to win the game
I got to stay patient
gotta stay the same
I can't give up now
I can't change
I must maintain and sustain
there's brighter days ahead
just gotta play the game
they took my queen from me
its hard to be the king

I've been influenced
corrupted
spiritually deducted
let me tell you what it is
to be abducted
psychologically reconstructed
deconstructed
destruction

I'm an existence
natural born resistence
to ignorance

The journey of Life
Stay the same you'll die
you must adapt to the weather
Different seasons different methods
Different reasons

Gotta keep it together
stay patient
To survive

Stop fooling yourself
You need to stop proving yourself
The law of the universe
You gotta give in order to receive
A misconception
Devious deception
When you associate success with foolery
Ignorance with jewelry
Jealousy, envy and hate
Ignorance is the culture
Spiritual hypocrisy
Accidents and investigations
People get the wrong impressions
They don't know
It was just a mistake

Life is like a blizzard
Watch out for snakes and lizards
Witches and wizards
I'm shivering
Because of this cold
I'm shivering
I'm on an expedition
Spiritual extradition
To figure out the meaning of life

Life is a shadow
An ongoing battle
In pursuit of pleasure

Its like drinking dirty water
Forever
Then you take a stop
And get a drop
You can't stop
You can't go back
To that filth

Life is a curse
Born in the worst
Spiritual thirst
I give you water
You want dirt
Dirt and water needs light
To produce life
The light and the life are lies
I exist as thirst

We are shadows of time
Shadow-boxing against life
Shades of grey, dark and ivory

Life is an excuse
To make a difference
A gradual process
of growth and development
And predicted preconceived notions

Life is like a daughter
The better you treat her
The more you teach her
The greater she'll become later
Life is like a daughter

I sabatage myself
I sabotage myself
ten steps away from wealth
two steps my date with death
I sabotage, I sabotage
I sabotage myself

There's nothing to be gained in life
It's a test
The propagation of flesh
The manifestation of the best
Yes
....

(66) Parts of Man

Delve deep into the furthest depths of the mind
where all your hopes and worries
are left behind
follow me through this journey
the paths of faith
in a land far away
now tell me what will you find
360 degrees beneath the flesh
360 degrees above the mind
look into your soul
your reason for existing
what do you believe
your thoughts and dreams
what will you achieve
up on this earth
bathe your mind in this knowledge

college
it seperates morning from night
what's wrong from right
death from life
from birth
and what we do on planet Earth
from what we do in our dreams
where we can be anything

what about your attitude
what abuot your principles
your values
your morals
ethical code
reasoning
historical being
ethnic origin
genetic potential
what about the things you never seen
that's part of you
what about happiness and joy
what about pleasure and pain
Envy and Gain
360 degrees above everything
you wanted to be
everything your eyes might see
take a step into your heart
and see what you'll find
it'll blow your mind
what you love and hate
charish, negate
take a peek into your soul
tell me what you'll find

Parts of Man: The Declaration of Truth

it separates man from beast
spirit from flesh
principles and creed
a beast will do anything
even defile your wife
they won't think twice

The mind holds knowledge
the body holds blood
the soul holds love
it also holds a grudge
it also holds hate
what part of yourself is most important
the mind, body, or soul
thats up to you to decide
I really don't know
without knowledge
you can't create
with a body
you procreate
make things manifest
without a soul
you can't love or hate
persue happiness
or have eternal life
the first step is the construction
of the flesh within the matrix
the second step is the construction
of the mind
the final step is the enhancesment
of the soul
growth and development
knowledge, wisdom and understanding

shining light on ignorance
triple darkness
deaf, dumb and blindness
living death

lost all your material weath
can't even pull up yourself
help yourself
stuck in a shallow grave
God pulled me up
you're playing checkers
I'm playing chess
I'm simply the best
....

(67) The Declaraton of Truth

Stop digging into the ground
what you want cannot be found
what you do has sets and bounds
Robbing God
forcing us to bow down to you
destroying people for the sake of you
poppa pope its 2 plus 2
who are you
I'm talking to
Mr. President
I don't see you

I am the thought that clouds your judgment
the bias which leads you astray
the fear that causes you to lose hope

I am doubt
I am the strength
that allows you to move forward
the glance you take when the sun first shines
day break
when its dark and cold,
I'm the imaginaiton of the sun and warmth
I am hope

the storms, the weather
winter and summer,
the dusk, the dawn,
the night, the fight,
wrong and right.
the seasons

I'm that last sip you take
when you have nothing else to drink
when you're thirsty and hungry
think of me
I'm that hour
when its time to sleep
when you're tired
think of me
I'm that feeling you get
after accomplishing a mission
think victory
think of me
think vengengence
think me

time is all in the mind
its like tug of war

between God and Satan
I'm a poem
....

(68) My Father

There's only certain people
in this world
who know what love is
You can compare that to what you have
They don't have nothing
You have something
But you don't have nothing
Because you didn't gain anything
You didn't give anything

There's only certain people
in this world
who know what love is
Who struggle to take care of their families
Who have little wealth
Lack great material possessions
But their prosperity will have abundances

I had a vision
A dream
Where I heard someone coming in the house
from the basement
Of my old home
Where my family had grown
I was frightened
I figured it was my brother or an intruder

I was shocked to see him
My father
Looked sad and lost
Like he was on a long journey
To find his way home
His jacket was wet
Familiar clothes
He looked at me
He finally found his way back home
I woke up
But I still feel he's alone
The world did him wrong

....

(69)

(In Dedication to the Late Monte I. Fateen)

Will you take this journey with me?

by Baheerah J. Fateen

As the vows are said and the oaths are read
On the solemn ground we now tread
Will you take this journey with me?
With joy, pain, hardship and strain
We will go out to face life
Together as husband and wife
Hand and hand, our hearts and spirits will land
To withstand the fears
And face the challenges of the years
Being steadfast
Not knowing how long the journey together
would last.
As we look back on the past

and remember how we look on the tiny faces
of our children when they were babies
As they lay on the tiny cradle-like places and
cramped spaces
And again when they are grown and gone
with children of their own.
As we journey on in time
Not knowing what we would find
With the tus that bind the people the places
the frowns and smiles
As we traveled the miles and unwritten files and
piles of words
Both good and bad, some even sad, but all sorted
out by time
Will you take this journey with me?
Who knew at the beginning of the journey what
we would find,
Happiness, sadness, or peace of mind
Like a fleeting burst of time
in that dreaded day of this journy we find
no more time to plan, no more places to see
the journey together is over.
when we stand or is layed
what will the one of us say
when in the presence of our family and friends
and other next of kin
not knowing how long our journey together
would last
it went away too fast
as time past I reflect and say
I am happy we chose each other
to take this journey

Parts of Man: The Declaration of Truth

together as husband and wife
through happiness and joy, sadness and pain,
even strife
and know this is the essence of life.

....

THE BOOK

of

LYRICS

by

Marwan Fateen

--------Part One--------

I.

I told poetry
please stay close to me
Me and you share a common destiny
You bring out the best in me
I told misery
Me don't want no parts of thee

Life is a conspiracy
Imagine if you were me
Rejected by society

We are born to die
We yearn to cry
Life teaches us why
Church preaches us lies

Life is a slide
Life is a tide
Life is a ride
I'm passing by
Life is something
You cannot buy

Hell naw another day
Will I choose to go away
Hell naw another day
Will we choose to go astray

II.

This little fly
Just flew in my eye
It wont make me cry
I know it won't die
But why did this fly
Just fly in my eye

Looked up
Time passed you by
Doing nothing
The difference between lyrics and life

Why do we wanna save people
Because saving them will save ourselves
Part of us is in them

You have to be
What you want them to be
Because they will be
Whatever you are

III.

She's Hot

She has the biology
The psychology
Spirituality
Astronomical qualities

She caused me to levitate
I didn't hesitate
Guarding your heart
Ducking these darts
This is my art
she's everything I need
she's hot

Spiritual seduction
I got abducted
By your beauty
First I was reluctant

The attraction
The interaction
Satisfaction
I love the way you stare
From your feet to your hair
That glare
Please share

IV.

God will bend the arrow in the air
we call them bullets
people used to try
now they're scared to pull it
to make God out a lie
many have tried but couldn't
they all fell by the way side

Nebucanezar to Greece
war and peace

V.

The moon don't move

I sit by this river
yet the moon don't move
my skin shifts and it shivers
it shakes, it quiivers
but the moon don't move
we dance and we groove
but when we looked up
the moon still don't move

VI.

You're destiny is doom and destruction
defiling each others' wives
the wicked is those who know right
but do evil
the hypocrite
the physical manifestation of Satan
ruined your own women
have respect for the next man
broken promises
To be a Black man with locks
they think we're criminals
Animals

The Ghetto Farm
I have social equality
I'm equipped
Society is orginaized Chaos

VII.

Mental Contamination

The mass media think your thoughts
its your fault
there's a direct correlation
between what you want
what you see
and what your body reacts to
if you don't like what you automatically react to
all you gotta do is think your own thoughts
as you thnk their thoughts in your heart
you are them
manufactured your mind
second captivity
train your mind and body
to react to something else
you do that by changing what your soul desires
everything that manifest in reality
originates in the mind

I'd appreciate some appreciation
I'm tired of the negative connotations
In the eyes of the world
we have become the epitome of wickedness

and filth
come back to your original self
or else
you'll suffer the consequence

VIII

Ignorance
there is no cure
but truth
the light
there is no power
but from God
the might
He has the power
there is no truer
Life is like a tree
Springing up from the darkness
Into light
Bearing fruit
Planting seeds
Repeating the cycle
Everlasting life
this square I'm standing on
Is bigger than your house
Principles and standards
Born with a cup of knowledge
now I'm in a sea of wisdom
headed to celestial bodies
of understanding
I'm too demanding

notwithstanding
the foundation of truth
its too big for this planet
Take off your tail
Stop living in hell

IX

Evryday I gotta face doom
death and destruction
When I go back to my neighborhood
Life is miserable
Drugs
Escape to cloud nine
Hide from reality temporarily
Until sobriety kicks in
Now you cant pretend
so you Just give n
Arabs own everythang
someone has to be the blame
political hypocrites
religious vagrants

X

This is my sequel
We all are equal
My Pocket book is from heaven
I'm not trying to do seven
hypocritical reverend

couldn't do nothing for Kevin

Crying in the bull pen
They gave him sixty years
Shouldn't have done what he did
If he had another chance
He wouldn't do it again
Only 18
Had the whole world ahead of him
Two lives gone
Now he's forgotten
But his story lives on

They said he snitched
Now he's in a ditch

XI

Life is about knowledge
If you're not learning
You're burning
Stop turning life into a wasteland
It's a crime

in dreams all things are possible
all knowleddge is available
we are amphibians
living a physical and spiritual life
the mind connects the two

Who I was is who I am

The truth doesn't change
It remains the same

By the power vested me
I set this decree

Life is a disagreement
Between good and bad
Happy and sad
As a man
you take a loss
Shake it off and move on

Relative Humidity
Spiritual burglary
Mental surgery
Commiting perjury

The square root of reality
The square root of man

XII

Virtues

You cant taste or touch it
But you need it
they come from the soul
Develope as part of your character
a Fortified structure
it Brings success

Patience, Dedication, Reliability
Integrity, Trustworthyness, Faith
Courtousy, Honesty, Respect
Silence, Reverence, Humility
Courage, Loyalty, Fairness
Without integrity, Tact
negotioation with respect
Combination

XIII

Me not grinding
Is like the sun not shining
Stop nagging me
Psychologically dragging me
FM frequency
Juvenile delinquency
Baptist churches and abortion clinics
The black women are always in it
I got to separate myself
From these skanks and witches
A metamorphisis
But I'm no Morpeius
He's dangling, straggling and strangling
Society's filled with mindless, spineless zombies
You're too impatient
Signed a contract with satan
A psychotic break
Mental destruction

XIV

Raped by her father and brother
no guidance from her mother
lost faith in the Holy Father
now she's Lucifer satan's daughter

a spiritual murderer
look what you done to her
you got a special place in Hell
she's going to be a woman one day
somebody's mother someday

he got molested
spiritually arrested
mentally suggested
tested

these niggas gotta die
pimping our women
molesting our children
ruining our future
these niggas gotta die

XV

Influence

Hierarchy of expected behavior
Based on skin tone and status
Psychologically defeated

You already lost

It must be against the law
To support ourselves
We abort ourselves
Bent on death and destruction
When you get an opportunity
Take it
I commit crimes against the mind
I repossess your soul from satan

XVI

Determination

They knock you down
But you got to get back up
Pull up from your bootstraps
Cast your bucket where you are
Get to work
Say's Booker T
Determination will take you far
Perseverance

The Deck is stacked against us
They don't care about us
So why care about them

All the troublemakers are gone
Dead or changed
Both one in the same
You're given the opportunity

To be the white man's slave
My people have no unity
But for money we behave
I'm not afraid of death
Because I know there's life after flesh

Carry yourself with respect and class
Don't bury yourself
By showing your a#$

Corporate slavery
So much captivity going on
Share those dividends with the people

Conducting experiments
Injected us with syphilis
Eugenics
Now its abortion clinics

I had a choice
Life or death
Change or stay the same

XVII

poverty the pimp
its a foregone conclusion
moral delimma
population control
sucking the blood
Abuse the people
Misuse the power

Mommas chose to do that dope
Crack babies
The beast
The enemy of humanity
The oppressor of society
We are too young to give up
I'm getting old
Ignorance is a castle
That we all build
The foundation is darkness
Its bricks are infinite
Holding off for next time
the most powerful word in the universe
is no
My faith is security
They got low self-esteem
so they compensate with money
cars and schemes
to compensate for their low self-esteem
they use them words
poverty is a pimp
Don't support businesses
Who rob and exploit your community
Genocide
Prison
Killing
The black man is under attack
Forgotten children
Coming up missing
Coming thru the cracks
Of pollution
Looking for the solution

Instant revolution
Without contribution
Strip joints and houses for the sodomites
Integration
More like disintegration

XVIII

The art of losing

Its lke looking at words
Without hearing a voice
Void of understanding

God is the Champion
Very close to me
Wherever I am
That's where I'm supposed to be

My block is kind of dangerous
Patches of hoodlums everywhere
You might not see me again

You're stuck in the mundane
You're stuck in this body
The vessel
The flesh

They're sucking our blood
Showing no love
Nobody knows where the money goes

To the liquor stores
So we can give them some more

I see the mother of harlots
The father of pimps

I wash myself of society

Treat it with kindness
The golden rule

Massahs dirty little secret
Satellite oppressors

Niggas on the porches
dreams of buying Porsches

Gotta go through the wilderness
Don't go back to Egypt

I'm not a worldy possession
I'm not

Pitiful petty people
Produce doom and destruction

We're dead until we find our true purpose
our calling

XIX

Addiction
to sex
To misery
To drama
To pain
To drugs and alcohol
Whatever it may be
It has your soul
You want to escape
to your mask, your cape
Can't deal with reality
You need help

There's going to be a time
When the men of God
Will have to fight the men of Satan

XX

Cut your dreds
Dreads are to be cut
I still got dreds
Internal
How can I cut these dreds

People coming back
Because they think they can
You gotta cut them dreds
Don't let em lock up again

I think life should be pleasant
Sometimes it takes going through hardships
Before that can happen

How do I cut theses dreds
Forgiveness
People I used to hang with
Were dreds
Had to cut them off

Those dreds had negative energy stored
I feel free

On a pursuit for something unattainable
Something incedible
Spiritually edible
Its unbelievable and achievable

XXI

The once queen of the universe
Has fallen
Messing with a white bag
Is like throwing up the white flag
You might as well wear a white mask
And hope to get your life back

they retreat to the white beat

I don't have a wife or relationship

Poetry is my mistress

is that what you see
when you look at me
idiot, clown, bafoonery
carrying someone elses child
then you come back to me
is that what you see

Peep the psychology
You only understand misery
It's the point where
You measure everything

XXIII

This night seems like eternity
I don't work for money
Money works for me

Money seems vain to me
I don't really need it
Money is a game to me

All work and no play
Is almost like slavery

Money is like a drug
The spending and splurging
Is the high

Jealousy, envy, hate
These are mechinisms
That control your fate

The physical body
Isn't the end all be all
Body isn't everything
because at some point
The clothes will come off

The body is a vehicle
The mind is a steering wheel
Just like we can worship
And make a car into a god
We can do the same with our bodies

I kind of feel sorry for those
Who have it easy

What would the day be without night
What would courage be
Without fight
We need someone to balance us out
Adam and Eve

I'm in the winderness
God is feeding me from Heaven
Until I reach the Promise Land

--------Part Two --------

XXIV

We are the children of the Most High...
we fear no man
we take a stand
all in the trust in His Master plan
144,00 will lead
will plead
while the rest will bleed

The LORD gave me wealth
wisdom and good health
gave me the tree of life
I eat from it
everything you desire to be
I become it
man can't get along with each other
due to the criminal behavior
sabotaging each other
stopping progress
causing pain and stress
regret
the day you left me wet
forgave but I did not forget

forces moving behind the scenes
indestructabile
spirits chasing behind me

anything's possible
A perpetual struggle
blessed by God
who else cares
about the Black man's struggle

XXV

Mild Sauce

as a child
I thought and acted like a child
As a man
No time for foolery
Don't mean to burst your bubble
But we're just stuck in the struggle
No choice but to hustle
Ignoring someone can cause
Psychological damange
When it hits me
How will I take it?
Devilish doctrine
Tryna sabotage my soul
My own women were never there for me
I'm messed up
Society raised me to be messed up
Niggas sicked a dog on me
Stop blaming the white man
For what you've done
That's not his child
That's your son

Who's acting wild
I'm not failing
I'm dwelling
Selling my poetry
Mentally stranded
Drugs, death and destruction
Menace to society
From Moses to Aphrodite
This pain I feel inside me
Came on as fast as lightning
Clothes, shoes and hair dos
Sitting on poverty's lap
Waiting on a scrap
Who threw a diamond in the gumbo?
Your brain is dangling
Want to be part of the fast life
The low life
The most beautiful thing
I've ever seen
Is an artistic mind
Creativity
If you can't accept who I am
Then why are you around me?
A day to die
Mentally maintained
Spiritually drained
The neighborhood is all in the mind
The thieves are in
What are you going to do
When the thieves are in
Your body is a commodity
When you think you're pretty

Long live the king
Society's mistress
I am the witness
Been dragging this bag for years
Found out
I don't have any peers
I'm flirting with death
This type of love should be a crime
But there's nothing else
Black hoes scrambling
Rambling
Psychologically gambling

XXVI

Its like seeing turtles
Without a shell

It's a must that we rest
To be the best
To past the test
To defeat the rest

You're on someone else's clock
Someone else's hour
Someone else has the power

Everything is a mentality
I'm society's administrator
A misdemeanor

Chocolate chips
The flavor of life
Would ice cream taste the same
Without fudge

Life is a pyramid scheme
Life is my occupation

A letter to your mind
Dear thoughts:

these woman don't really care about us
I don't understand it
Emotionally stranded
Psychologically disbanded
I really can't stand it

Orchard
I got psychologically tortured
Holding off for next time
you must know any oppressor of this strife life
so you'll be able to build on these hills

XXVII

Hierarchy of expected behavior
Based on skin tone and status
Psychologically defeated
You already lost
It must be against the law

To support ourselves
We abort ourselves
Bent on death and destruction

When you get an opportunity
Take it
I commit crimes against the mind
I repossess your soul from Satan
And put it back into the hands of God

To be scared is to be dead
Because fear comes from ignorance
And ignorance is darkness
And darkness is death
Face your fears
You're enslaved to your fear

Stop smoking up the cash
Putting it in an ash tray
Dollars to ashes
Ashes to dust

The culture is a living entity
False dreams come out
Manufactured by society

True happiness is unchangeable
Priceless
If you lose all of your things
You still have it

Talk to the watchmen
If they don't listen
Its up to the lenchmen

Society deem me a bum and a failure
Because there's no loyalty or support
You're a traitor

I don't worship your beauty
Or praise your flesh, your body
A relationship can't be based on flesh
Bow down praising the Lord
To the flesh

XXVIII

Critical thinking

You're imprisoned
To your five senses
On top of the roof
Hiding

A man took
What God had prepared for me
A man took
What God provided for me
Did he really take it
Or did I just give it away?

I want to be good

But I have barriers
Protecting my heart
I have Fortified fortresses
Protecting my heart

They boast their bafoonery with pride
They wear their ignorance
Like a badge of honor
Incorporated, accepted, and expected stupidity
All these fools waiting on life
Go get it

XXIX

Walk off
you'll live longer
you'll be free longer
just walk off
the problems will be solved

Sometimes we say too much
When we should just say enough
Because too much is not enough

the power of faith
taking command of the ether

I wish I had pictures to show you
from all the places I've been
things I've done
people who became friends

but I don't
all I have is words
coming from the bottom of my pen
I didn't think about exploiting them
when it happened

our women focus too much
on thier outter appearance
like dressed up dolls
they need ot focus on their inner selves
and recognize true beauty comes from within

you catch hell
where the niggas dwell
who are the niggas?
is it you?

find out who the best is
and do it better than him

reality pulled up
jumped out
this is me

as long as you exist in my heart and thoughts
the dream isn't gone
I'm not alone
we will come home
on the Most High's throne

XXX

they keep telling me
wait til I get back
I'm waithing and waiting
but they seldom come back

they say
Marwan is a bum
he's on the streets
selling poetry
they say

you were there when I needed you
showed care
irregardless of how I treated you
unconditional love

there is no resistence
to the power, authority
of my throne
its better left alone
who do you want to be
what do you strive to see
when will you get there
or do you travel by mind
travel my mind

I see men break down
lose their minds
go crazy

stop drinking
start thinking
some need the drink to think
some need to think to drink

they told me get self-control
I looked into my soul
lo and behold
I found you
you are who
I am you

XXXI

its all about male and female
reproduction
spiritual selection
evolution
the only institution
everything else
an illusion

psychological adreniline
 a mental boost
God will protect the innocent
so I speak the truth
the rest is up to you

the woman used me
seduced me outta my money
made me pay for the honey

she introduced me
Got the right to be as wicked as you wanna be
wicked independent woman

XXXII

God has been good to me
Bullets could have penetrated me
but the LORD stood next to me
those bullets hit my back
then went around me
they almost cracked my skull
God pulled me back
coulda slit my wrist
you were there for me
waging war for me
Thank you God
for saving me

scared of what might become of me
I'm walking in

To die is to be everything
everywhere
but at the same time nothing
to live is to be nothing
nowhere
but at the same time something
becoming

XXXIII

all I want is knowledge
impulsiveness

subconscious condition
without your awareness
your body reacts to what you see and hear
you're programmed outside your awareness
a perpetual state of fear
no one near

metamorphing
without realizing
you're commiting genocide
against your own identity

don't succumb to flesh
overcome the flesh
there's more to life than flesh

how to control your emotions

the world is of the mind
the mind has dominion over physical reality
and the spirit has control over the mind

the purest writings come
when you stop listening to everyone else
and look within yourself

they always want something
but when you need them
you can't give anything
should you be like them
misuse and abuse others
or just be yourself

individualism,
all you care about is self
nothing else

selfishness,
all you care about is self
nothing else

--------Part Three --------

XXXIV

God has made Himself known to me
sent His angels to protect me
and guide me in the right direction

God put me in this situation
just so I can learn a lesson
to keep me from socond guessing
I'm steady counting my blessings

choose God over lust
choose God over sin
God so loved the world
he gave his only Son
to raise you from the dead
you wont just eat off bread
the tree of life
that will be fed

praise the Lord
with all your heart
don't pretend in church
to please men
God knows your heart
cheap fame will come to not

Come to God

or go to satan
the lake of fire
or dwell in Heaven
Christ conquered satan

turn to God
man will let you down
turn to God
everything else has failed

Thou will shall be done
on earth
as it is in Heaven
the resurrection
can this dead flesh live
can these dry bones breath
God gave the breath of life
believe
the resurrection
correction
make the blind man see
the deaf to hear
the dumb to speak

the flesh needs the spirit
my people don't want to ear it
we praise being sinners

the spirit against the flesh
death against the life
Christ did conquer twice

follow what Christ did
what is right
not wickedness
don't excuse committing sin

XXXV

I sit and pray
I dream of this day
there's no escape
meet your fate
the lies, the hate
yall have your day
all the things you done
I coulda killed you
you on my line
doing good and living free
the sweetest revenge
my teeth clinge
the sweetest revenge
look at you, look at me
the sweetest revenge can be

the sweetest revenge
is forgiveness and doing well
my success is the sweetest revenge

XXXVI

counter criminals
you can't save money when its in your pocket
stop looking for the expiration date

For a couple of these
They're bound to do anything

Every woman wants a knight in shining armor
to save them from the fire breathing dragon

Everyone has a solution
But I'm just here to listen

Those who need kudos and recognition
for everything they do
aren't real
If it's real
they'll put it out there anyway

XXXVII

It's too late

everyone you used to date
everyone you used to hate
it's too late
who you went to school with
thought you were cool with
it's too late

everyone you wanted to date
its too late
you used me too escape
its too late

XXXVIII

What is life
A formal introduction
Animated death
Death is life

does the sun gets tired of shining
The poet gets tired of rhyming
The hustler gets tired of grinding
Or does the preacher gets tired of lying

We praise and reward corruption
We praise low lives and criminals
A race of murderers drug dealers and failures
No escape
hell inside
hell outside
Niggas are like a snowball
rolling down a mountain
With each passing moment
The destruction gets bigger faster
Until its inevitable crash

If women treated relationships like their job
They'd be happy

To lose is to gain
And to gain is to lose

Enemies become your friends
While your frends lol

Watch the ones who are always smiling
The tongue is a deadly destructive device
defiling

Wisdom and knowledge

Life is more than just looks
Life is a struggle
A tussle
A hustle

XIL

The nigga farm
but I have the key
unlock your mind
endless possibilities

10 steps away from wealth
2 steps my date with death
I sabotage
I sabotage
I sabotage myself
I sabotage life

I sabotage death
Mental physical spiritual health
Ten steps away from wealth
Two steps my date with death
I'm sabotaged

XL

Ms. right?
Who is she
All I know is Ms. wrong
Ms. Donky kong
Jadde life in a thong

Misery speaks to me

My arms are shaking
I'm tryna figure out
Who burned the bacon

Theres no such thing as nothing
Nothing is ignorance
you either know or you dont

How did you go from being happy as a child
To this
Did the world let you down
Did society let you down
Did your mom let you down
Did I let you down
or did you let yourself down

your own expectations

The struggle from outside

What is life without honor
What is death without substance
Limbo

I'm supposed to be down
I'm supposed to be in the ground
I'm supposed to be locked up 6 x 9 underground
but I'm down town

XLI

I protest against my fate everyday
I protest against my fate everyday

I want to be the example
For your eyes to see
I want to be the change
For your mind to be

Life is a social construct
Life is the question
art is the answer
Life is the problem
art is the solution

Oblivious
They're so oblivious

We're symbolic beings
theories, ideas,
abstract living entities
inhabiting physical bodies
Manufactured mentality
Falsification of reality
The culture is a living entity
False dreams come out
Manufactured by society

True happiness is unchangable
Priceless
If you lose all of your things
You still have it

Life is about conquering satan
Faith is making the impossible possible
Imagination made real
The placebo effect

I figured out the meaning of life
There's only one thought/mind
Divided into different bodies
When we die
We are part of a celestial body
of spirit

XLII

messing with these gold diggers
might jeapardise your life
they want you low down
dirty, trifling and strife
druggin' and thuggin'
murdering madness
don't need no education
no occupation
or you'll get left stranded

I'm homeless
I'm homeless
I got a place to live
but I still feel homeless

they turned my women into
whores and sluts
groves and gluts
holes in ruts
in huts

XLIII

they're pilliging the planet
for the sake of the profits
corporations

what I've been told
there's no such thing as cold

or old

the only time I get heat
is when I go to sleep

I'm that invigoraing
feeling you get
to escape
run as fast as you can
trying to be free

who I was
is who I am
the truth don't change

it remains the same

depriving yourself
of your wants and needs
feeds your spirit
the self isn't the body
but the ideas
that makes up the person

I believe in creating my own dreams

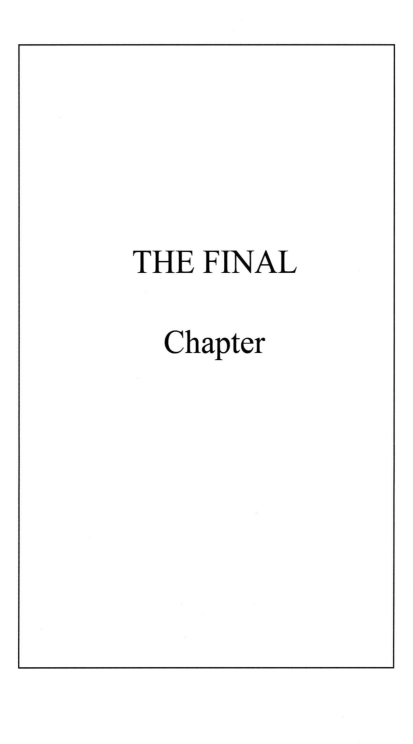

THE FINAL

Chapter

How I write poetry

I've been writing for most of my life.
When I was a very young child, maybe three-years-old, I would look at objects in the house, the tv, refridgerator, etc. and drew those objects as people and showed them to my mother. I took and idea and antropromorphisized it. This was the beginning of my life-long journey to understand life, reality, the world and everything else and convey it in simple language everyone can relate to and understand. I will attempt to teach you this technique in a couple of minutes.

-Create a topic or idea.
ponder that idea as long as it takes;
minutes, hours, even days.
only write when you get an epiphany after think-ing about that idea.
It might be one line, or five but write them down.
-The next epiphany might take hours or days of more thought, or just living life with that thought or idea in the back of your mind but when you get another one, based on inspiration, or whatever write it down!
-Keep doing this until you feel you have enough to properly convey your idea.
The beauty of this long process is, the time it took the come up with each epiphany will be evident to the reader, it will make your poem much richer than it would otherwise be with less time.
A poem that took an hour to write wouldn't have

as much depth as a poem that took months to create.

-The time inbetwee epipanies and lyrics will represent concentrated thought between the lines. Therefore, those days or months of thought between lines will be subconsciously absorbed by the reader and can be extracted or deduced or deconsentrated. For example, they would wonder what made you go from this idea to the next. That gap will be reasoned and deduced by them out of curiosity. This is how I write some of my literature.

-Only write when writing is the only way you can express yourself. Imagine your paper as your audience and your pen the speaker. Talk the the paper when you have problems, ideas, issues. Make your paper your best friend. That person you tell your deepest secrets too. Make your paper your most trusted ally. Talk to the paper and become the pen.

You are the pen, I am the paper. Talk to me.